WHAT WILL I SEE IN BRAZIL?

Geography for Kids

Children's Explore the World Books

D1523002

BABY PROFESSOR
EDUCATION KIDS

Speedy Publishing LLC

40 E. Main St. #1156

Newark, DE 19711

www.speedypublishing.com

Copyright 2017

Brazil is an enormous, beautiful country that is located in South America, and takes up most of the continent. The weather is tropical and the terrain is mostly flat, with some rolling lowlands to the north of the country. In this book, we will be learning about some of the amazing attractions this country has to offer.

BRASÍLIA – THE CAPITAL

B rasília was just developed by Lúcio Costa and Oscar Niemeyer in early 1956 and was formally proclaimed in April of 1960 as the capital of Brazil. It is known to be the world's largest city that did not exist at the start of the 20th century. It hosts the Brazilian Government as well as the headquarters of many Brazilian companies.

PALACIO DA ALVORADA EXTERIOR

There is so much to see and do in this city: walk the shore of Lake Paranoá, see the Square of Three Powers, enjoy gorgeous views from the Palácio da Alvorada (Palace of Dawn), or take your car and tour the Embassy Sector, which hosts 124 foreign embassies.

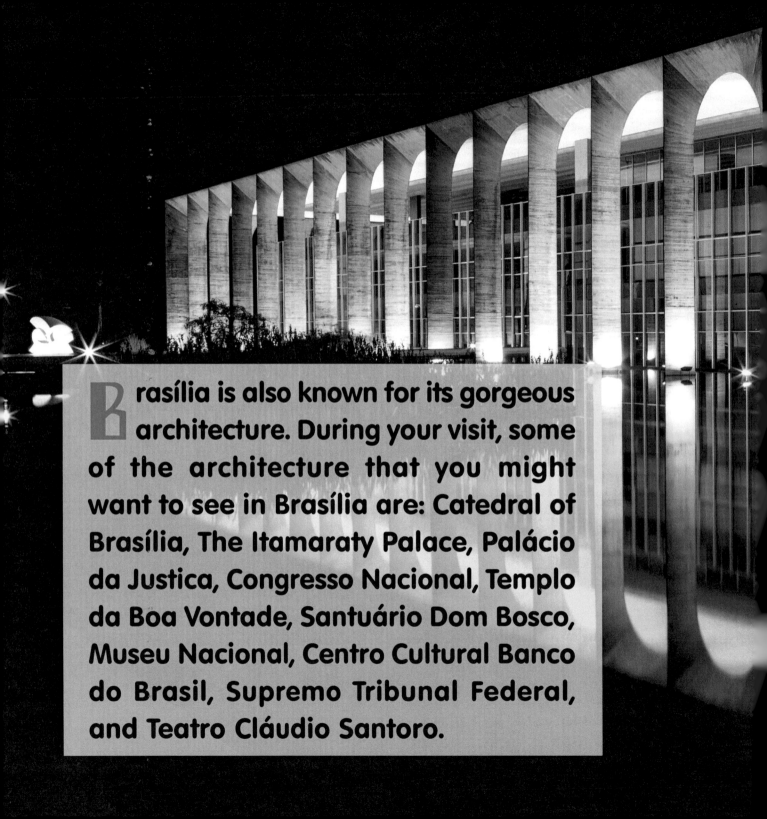

Brasília is also known for its gorgeous architecture. During your visit, some of the architecture that you might want to see in Brasília are: Catedral of Brasília, The Itamaraty Palace, Palácio da Justica, Congresso Nacional, Templo da Boa Vontade, Santuário Dom Bosco, Museu Nacional, Centro Cultural Banco do Brasil, Supremo Tribunal Federal, and Teatro Cláudio Santoro.

ITAMARATY PALACE

CHRIST THE REDEEMER STATUE ON CORCOVADO MOUNTAIN

This is one of the more popular attractions in Brazil. The statue of Jesus Christ, which is located in Rio de Janeiro, is at the peak of Corcovado mountain and his face fronts Sugar Loaf. The statue is 98 feet tall and is known to be the world's second largest Art Deco sculpture.

It was created between 1922 and 1931 by Paul Landowski, a Polish-French sculptor and built by Heitor da Silva Costa, a Brazilian engineer, along with Albert Caquot, the French engineer, using soapstone and reinforced concrete. This amazing statue is considered as an icon of Rio de Janeiro and is one of the New Seven Wonders of the World. Tourists can visit the top and have an amazing view of the city.

AERIAL VIEW OF AMAZON RAINFOREST, BRAZIL

THE AMAZON RAINFOREST

The world's largest rainforest, the Amazon Rainforest, is located on the Amazon River Basin in Brazil. The river basin is about the size of the 48 contiguous United States, and covers approximately 40% of the continent of South America, including parts of these eight countries: Bolivia, Brazil, Ecuador, Peru, Venezuela, Columbia, Guyana, and Suriname, as well as French Guiana, which is a department of France.

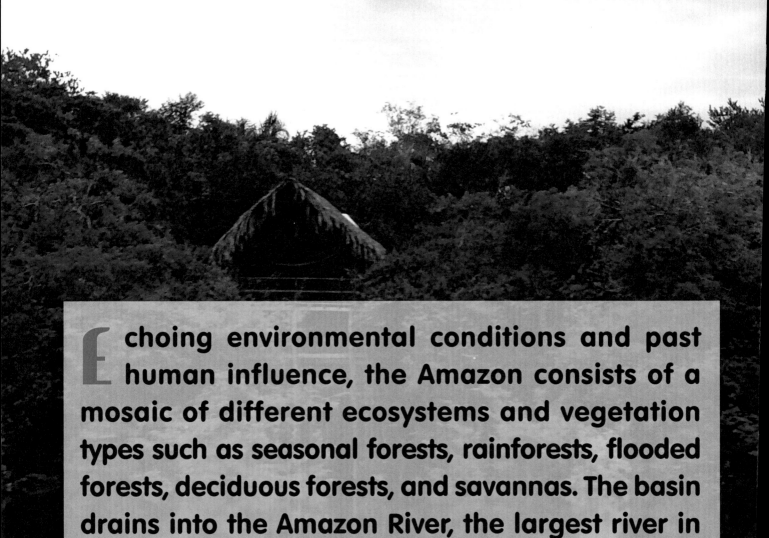

Echoing environmental conditions and past human influence, the Amazon consists of a mosaic of different ecosystems and vegetation types such as seasonal forests, rainforests, flooded forests, deciduous forests, and savannas. The basin drains into the Amazon River, the largest river in the world as far as discharge, and is second to the Nile River as the world's longest river.

WOODEN BUNGALOWS, AMAZON RIVER, BRAZIL

ANAVILHANAS NATIONAL PARK ISLANDS,
RIO NEGRO, BRAZILIAN AMAZON

It consists of more than 1,100 tributaries, of which 17 are more than 1,000 miles long, and two which are larger (the Madeira and the Negro), in terms of volume, than the Congo River, formerly known as the Zaire River. The forest's lifeline is this massive river system and its history plays a tremendous role for the development of the rainforests.

CARNIVAL OF BRAZIL

This annual festival is held each year between the Friday afternoon that occurs 51 days before Easter and noon on Ash Wednesday, marking the start of Lent, which is the 40-day period before Easter. Roman Catholics as well as other Christians abstain from eating meat and poultry. The word "carnival" is from the word "carnelevare", which means "to remove (literally, "raise") meat".

CARNAVAL PARADE PARTICIPANTS

CHILD HAVING FUN AT CARNIVAL IN BRAZIL

Carnival is arguably the most famous Brazilian holiday and has become an event of great proportions. Other than industrial production, carnival-related businesses, and retail establishments, Brazil completely unifies for about a week with festivities that are intense, night and day, mainly within the coastal cities.

THE IGUAZU FALLS

This is an amazing place to visit located at the border of Argentina and Brazil. Iguazu, or Iguaçu Falls are considered by the New Seven Wonders of The World Foundation as one of the brand New Seven Wonders of Nature, and can be found in the Rio Iguaçu, Brazilian state of Paraná. This attraction can be viewed from both Brazil and Argentina and are wider than the US Niagara Falls as well as the Victoria Falls in Africa.

IPANEMA BEACH IN RIO DE JANEIRO

RIO DE JANEIRO BEACHES

The Rio Beaches will provide you much fun in the sun! Some of the favorites that you won't want to miss are the Copacabana, Ipanema and Leblon beaches. If you want to take a stroll, you might want to visit Avenida where you can walk around and not have to worry about any trouble since they provide security. Even further is Praia do Arpoador, which is a great place for surf and prime location for watching the local surfers.

MORRO DE SÃO PAULO - BAHIA

This is another terrific Brazilian place to visit. It is one of five villages of the Tinharé islands, located in the northwest section of Brazil, about two hours from Salvador. A great way to visit is by catching a boat from the city of Valença, or catch a plane from Salvador to a small airport at the Morro de São Paulo Island.

A few nice things to note: cars here are not permitted, so prepare to enjoy lots of the natural environment! Its beaches are quite fancy and named First, Second, Third and Fourth beach, which makes them easy to find.

VIEW OF THE FIRST, SECOND AND THIRD BEACH

SUGARLOAF MOUNTAIN

Sugarloaf Mountain, with its summit reaching 1,300 feet above Guanabara Bay, offers gorgeous views of the beautiful landscape below consisting of a city that is crammed amongst the forest-covered peaks and the golden beaches adorned by turquoise seas.

SUGARLOAF MOUNTAIN, RIO DE JANEIRO, BRAZIL

UNDERWATER ARCH IN FERNANDO DE NORONHA

FERNANDO DE NORONHA

This is a must see if you enjoy scuba diving as it is known to be one of the world's most amazing sites for diving. Fernando de Noronha is an archipelago of 21 islands in the Atlantic Ocean, with terrific visibility in the waters. Unless you want to take a two-day cruise, the only way to reach these islands is by plane.

BEACH IN FERNANDO DE NORONHA BRAZIL

Additionally, it is a UNESCO World Heritage Site, and if you want to go inside, each day you will have to pay a minimal environmental preservation fee, but it is well worth it.

PANTANAL ISLAND

Pantanal is located in western Brazil, extending into Bolivia, and is known as one of the most diverse and largest freshwater wetland ecosystems in the world.

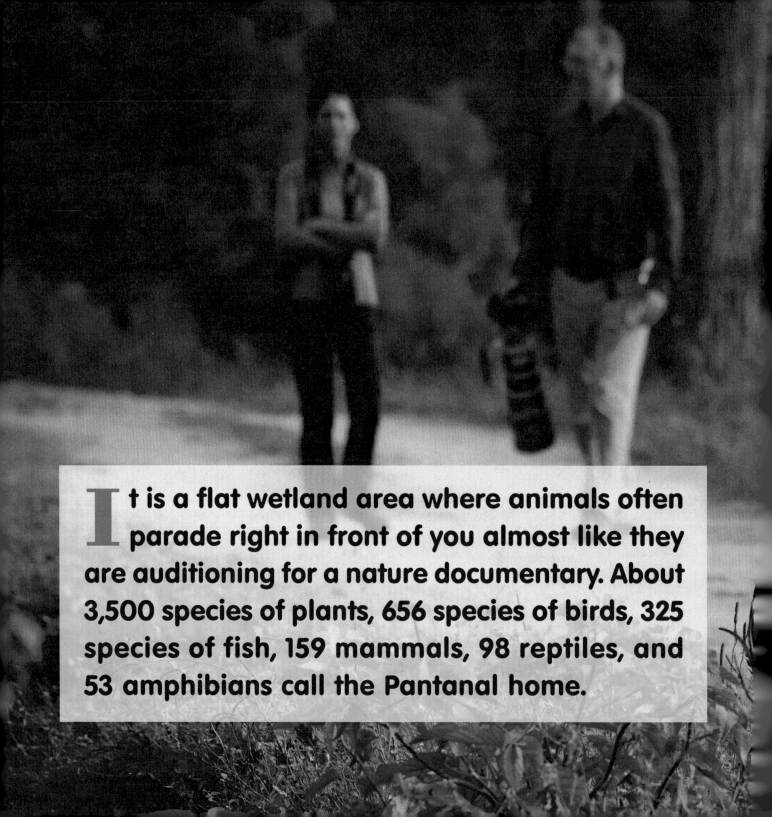

It is a flat wetland area where animals often parade right in front of you almost like they are auditioning for a nature documentary. About 3,500 species of plants, 656 species of birds, 325 species of fish, 159 mammals, 98 reptiles, and 53 amphibians call the Pantanal home.

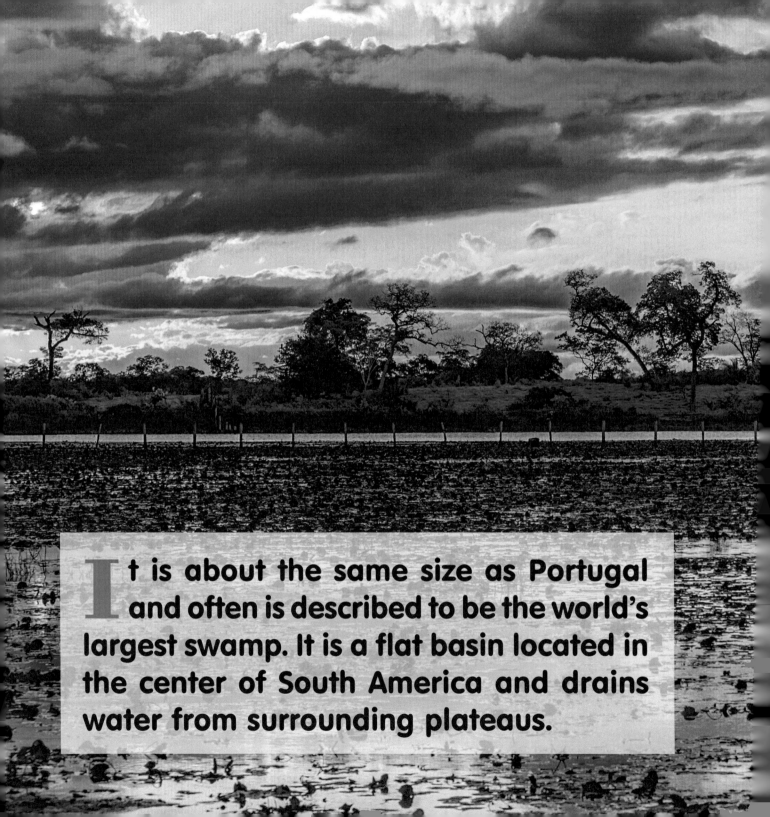

It is about the same size as Portugal and often is described to be the world's largest swamp. It is a flat basin located in the center of South America and drains water from surrounding plateaus.

HERD OF CATTLE, PANTANAL

For over a hundred years, the only human activity taking place has been the low-level ranching of cattle. However, raising cattle is in Pantanal is not competitive due to the landscapes constantly shifting in recent years and several ranches have closed and reopened as tourist lodges.

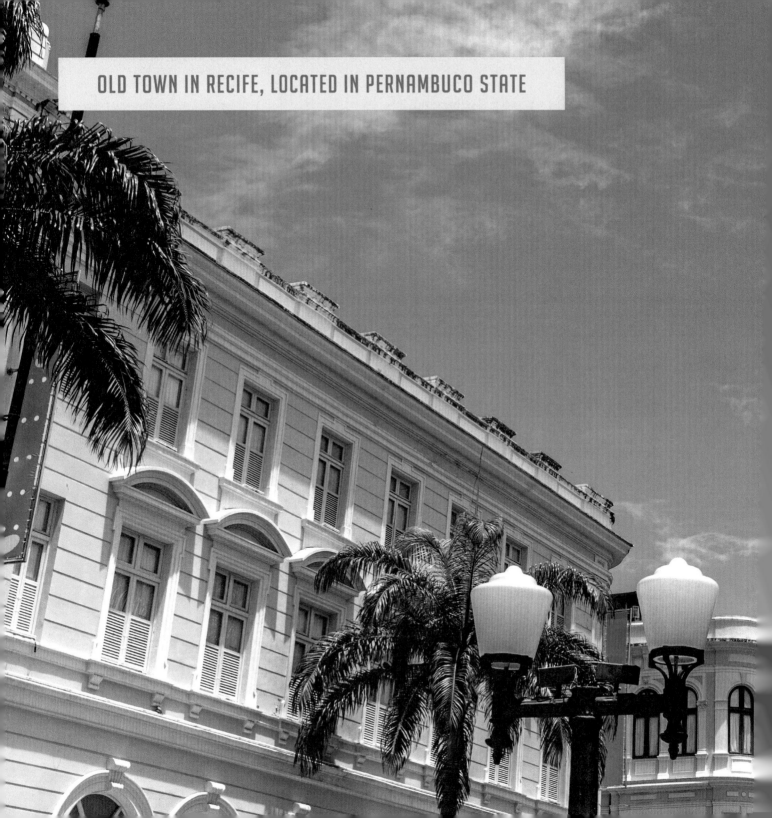

OLD TOWN IN RECIFE, LOCATED IN PERNAMBUCO STATE

HISTORIC CENTER OF OLINDA

Located in Pernambuco state is the Historic Center of Olinda. The preservation of this site started back in the 1930s, when major monuments became listed as national heritage sites.

SAO BENTO MONASTERY IN OLINDA, PERNAMBUCO

There have been several actions since then for preservation of the cultural, historical, and architectural heritage of this municipality. Olinda features several major tourist attractions including the historic downtown area, the Carnival of Olinda, and churches.

While the Carnival is similar to the carnivals in Rio de Janeiro and Salvador, there is no admission fee to attend the Carnival in Olinda. The festivities are all celebrated in the streets with no roping or bleachers and there are many small musical groups performing music in different genres.

CARNIVAL DANCER IN STREET PARADE

VILLAGE OF JERICOACOARA, CEARA, BRAZIL

JERICOACOARA - CEARÁ

Jericoacoara is located in the Brazilian northwest state of Ceará. The small town with sand streets is known as one of the more beautiful places to see in Brazil and there is plenty to enjoy.

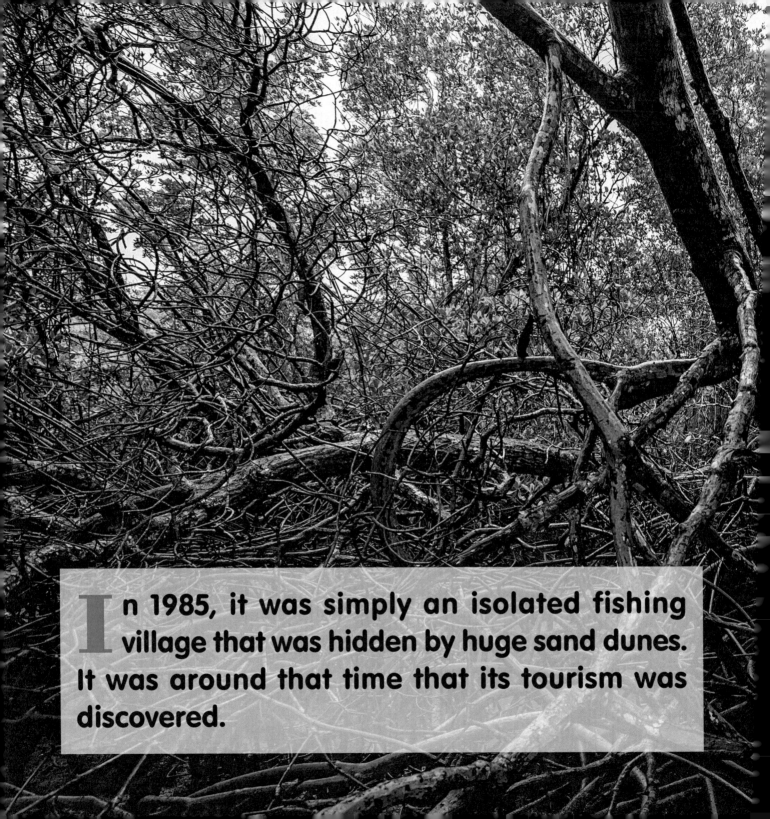

In 1985, it was simply an isolated fishing village that was hidden by huge sand dunes. It was around that time that its tourism was discovered.

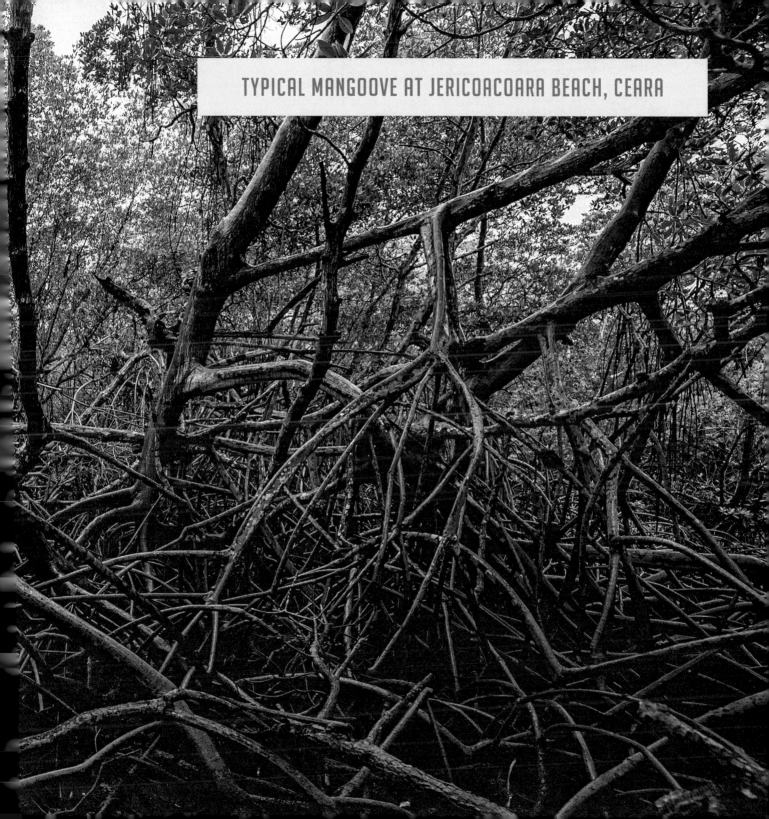

TYPICAL MANGOOVE AT JERICOACOARA BEACH, CEARA

DUNES OF JERICOACOARA

Located between the sea and large sand dunes, and being a peninsula, it is one of the few places in Brazil that you can watch the sun rise over the ocean.

There are several lakes and lagoons consisting of rain sweet water that are a must see on your trip!

These are only a few of the amazing attractions that Brazil has to offer. For additional information, you can go to your local library, research the internet, and ask questions of your teachers, family, and friends.

Visit

BABY PROFESSOR
EDUCATION KIDS

www.BabyProfessorBooks.com

to download Free Baby Professor eBooks
and view our catalog of new and exciting
Children's Books

Made in United States
North Haven, CT
28 February 2023